Guest Spot

CLASSICAL FAVOURITES
Playalong *for* Flute

T0078718

Order No. AM984467

Arranging and Engraving supplied by Camden Music.
Edited by Ann Farmer.
Cover photography by George Taylor.
Printed in EU.

CDs recorded, mixed and mastered by Jonas Persson.
Instrumental solos by John Whelan.
Piano: Tau Wey

ISBN: 978-1-84609-308-1

To acces audio visit:
www.halleonard.com/mylibrary

3159-9467-1852-4769

Visit Hal Leonard Online at
www.halleonard.com

Contact us:
Hal Leonard
7777 West Bluemound Road
Milwaukee, WI 53213
Email: info@halleonard.com

In Europe, contact:
Hal Leonard Europe Limited
42 Wigmore Street
Marylebone, London, W1U 2RY
Email: info@halleonardeurope.com

In Australia, contact:
Hal Leonard Australia Pty. Ltd.
4 Lentara Court
Cheltenham, Victoria, 3192 Australia
Email: info@halleonard.com.au

Guest Spot

A Musical Joke (Presto), K522 *Mozart* 7

Air (from 'The Water Music') *Handel* 12

Allegretto Theme
(from Symphony No. 7) *Beethoven* 14

Ave Maria *Schubert* 16

Entr'acte (from 'Rosamunde') *Schubert* 18

Jerusalem *Parry* 19

Jesu, Joy Of Man's Desiring *Bach* 20

Largo (from 'Xerxes') *Handel* 22

March (from 'The Nutcracker Suite')
Tchaikovsky 24

O For The Wings Of A Dove *Mendelssohn* 27

Sarabande (from Suite XI) *Handel* 30

Flute Fingering Chart 4

Flute Fingering Chart

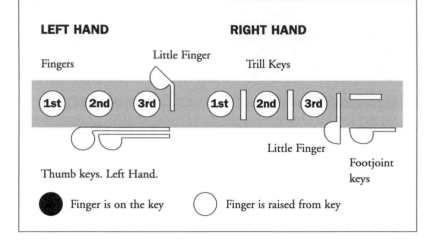

LEFT HAND · RIGHT HAND

Fingers · Little Finger · Trill Keys

1st · 2nd · 3rd · 1st · 2nd · 3rd

Little Finger · Footjoint keys

Thumb keys. Left Hand.

● Finger is on the key ○ Finger is raised from key

LEFT HAND · RIGHT HAND

C

C#/Db

D

D#/Eb

E

Same fingering for both notes

F

Same fingering for both notes

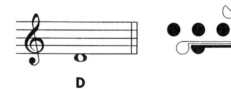

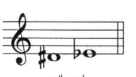

LEFT HAND · RIGHT HA

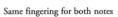

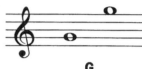

F#/Gb

Same fingering for both notes

G

Same fingering for both notes

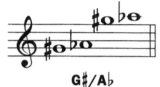

G#/Ab

Same fingering for both notes

A

Same fingering for both notes

A#/Bb

Same fingering for both notes

B

Same fingering for both notes

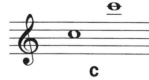

C

Same fingering for both notes

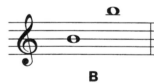

C#/Db

Same fingering for both notes

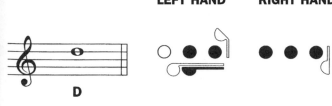

D

D♯/E♭

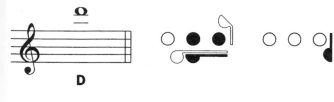

D

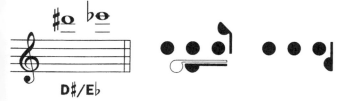

D♯/E♭

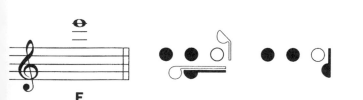

E

F

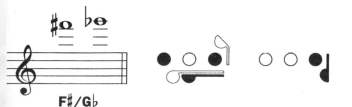

F♯/G♭

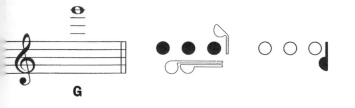

G

LEFT HAND   **RIGHT HAND**

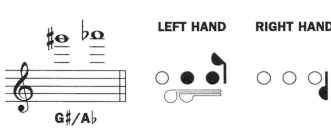

G♯/A♭

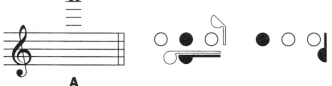

A

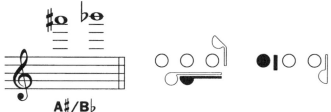

A♯/B♭

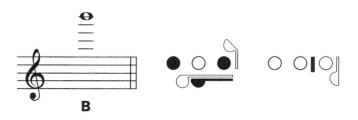

B

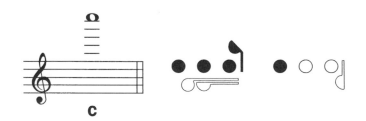

C

A Musical Joke (Presto), K522

Composed by Wolfgang Amadeus Mozart

f

p

p

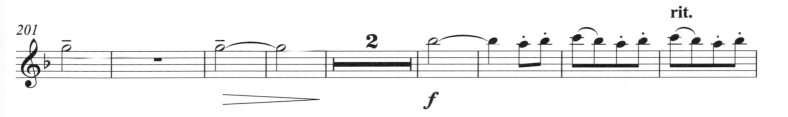

rit.

f

D.S. al Coda
(without repeats)

a tempo

p

⊕ Coda

f

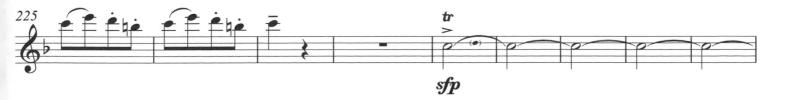

sfp

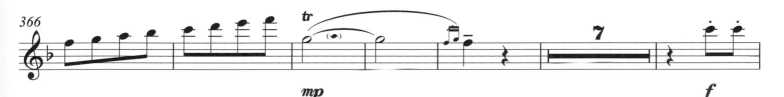

Air (from 'The Water Music')

Composed by George Frideric Handel

Moderato

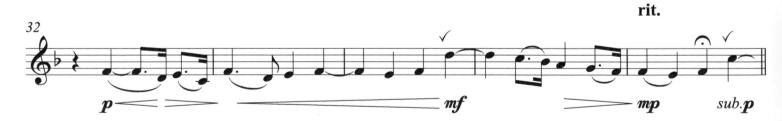

a tempo

Allegretto Theme (from Symphony No.7)

Composed by Ludwig van Beethoven

Ave Maria

Composed by Franz Peter Schubert

Lento (♩ = 72)

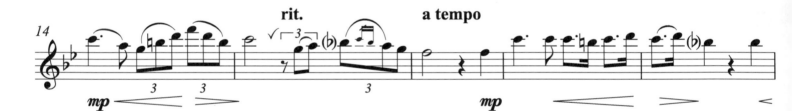

rit.   a tempo

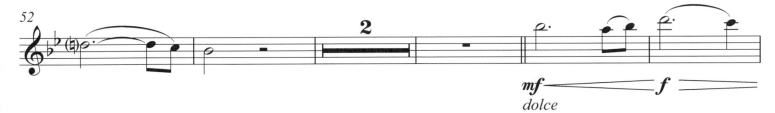

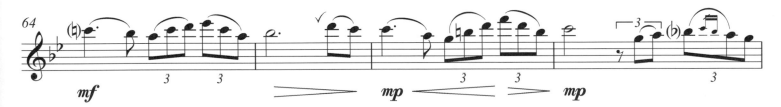

rit.   a tempo   rit.

Entr'acte (from 'Rosamunde')

Composed by Franz Peter Schubert

Jerusalem

Composed by Hubert Parry

Jesu, Joy Of Man's Desiring

Composed by Johann Sebastian Bach

Moderato (♩ = 76)

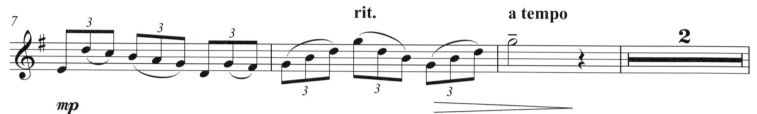

a tempo

a tempo, slower

rit. poco a poco

Largo (from 'Xerxes')

Composed by George Frideric Handel

Largo ($\quarternote = 60$)

rit.   a tempo

March (from 'The Nutcracker Suite')

Composed by Pyotr Ilyich Tchaikovsky

Tempo di marcia (♩ = 144)

O For The Wings Of A Dove

Composed by Felix Mendelssohn

Con moto (♩ = 69)

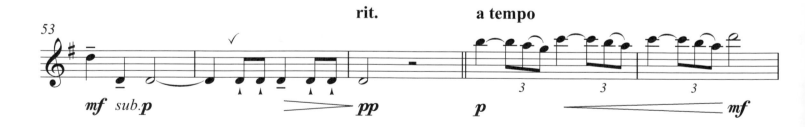

cresc.　　　　　　　　　　　　　　　　　　　　f　———————　p　　　　　　mp

mf　———　mp　　　　　　　　　　3　　　3　　f　—　mf　<

f　　　　　　　　　　　　　　　　p　　　　　　　　　　　　　　<

f　　　　　　　　　　　　　　　　p

rit.

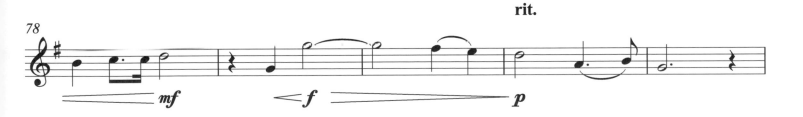

———　mf　　<　f　———————　p

a tempo

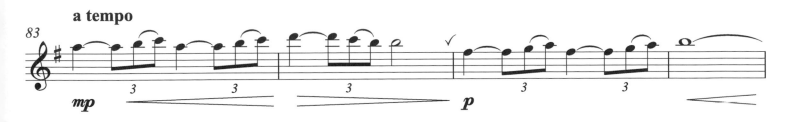

mp　3　　　3　　　3　　　　p　3　　　3　　<

rit.　　　**a tempo**

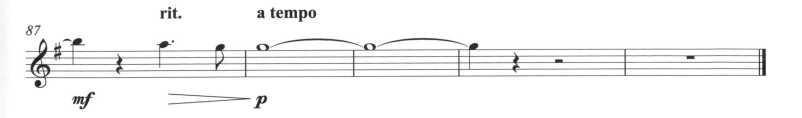

mf　　　———　p

Sarabande (from Suite XI)

Composed by George Frideric Handel

Lento (♩ = 72)

rit.

a tempo

rit.

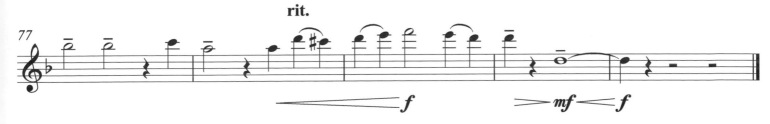